Remember —

Life is what we
make it... So ... let's
make it a "HUGE" life.

J.C. Men.

"I Think
I Smell
Garlic"

A RECIPE FOR LIFE

"I Think I Smell Garlic"

A Recipe for Life

J. C. Melvin

Ryan Ave Publishing

Copyright © J. C. Melvin 2004
All rights reserved
Second Printing

ISBN: 0-9760759-0-3
Library of Congress Control Number: 2004096491

Published By:
Ryan Ave Publishing Company
5738 Hedgeford Court, Top Floor
Las Vegas, NV 89120-2554

To order additional copies of this publication,
go to JCMelvin.com

Illustrations by Clem McCarthy
Editor: Annabelle Johnston
Book Jacket design by: Lisa Liddy, The Printed Page

To my loving wife
Minnie Keenan Melvin

Contents

Introduction

I Think I Smell Garlic is a recipe for life that was developed after a deep self-assessment of my business and personal life. In my career as a salesman, trainer, manager and speaker, I've talked to thousands of people concerning their dreams, visions, and goals. It's quite interesting to find that the common detractors keeping people from achieving their goals are very similar.

In my case, I found that a lack of organizational skills was affecting my business, my decision making, and the vision of my future. This guide is a result of that self assessment and I gladly share those truths and conclusions with you in the following chapters.

I had a burning desire to find the answers to why and what was stopping me from achieving my dreams and reaching my goals! This passion has been echoed by many over the years, but until now a simple "recipe for life" with a formula to find the answers has not been available.

The title of this book reflects the story of a frog (amazing creatures, very adaptable to their surroundings) unmotivated to save its own life primarily because it doesn't realize that its life is in jeopardy. It's said that if you were to place a frog into a pot of cool water and turn on the stove to a low heat the frog would adapt to the increasing heat until the water comes to a boil killing the frog.

Imagine for a moment that an instant before death the frog comes to the realization that it's about to be cooked for dinner. The smell of garlic permeates the air, but it's too late for it to survive. While we sometimes find ourselves in hot water, unlike the frog, it's never too late for us to jump out of the pot!

However, we are also quite adaptable and from time to time allow ourselves to be influenced by our surroundings, environment, friends and family. This guide will provide some tips for determining if you are in the pot, how to get out, and stay out. It is designed to deal with procrastination, decision making, attitude, motivation and the power of choice.

It's a guide about jumping out of the pot and living life to your fullest potential. It will guide you in unlocking your spiritual and emotional passion and assist you in clarifying your life's goals!

The Nuts and Bolts of the Guide

The guide which is subtitled "A Recipe for Life" provides a formula to accomplish your dreams and reach your goals!

The self awareness chapter will assist you in an honest evaluation of self, so that you can establish where you are today and create a starting point for your tomorrow. It is a "be honest" chapter which suggests that the more honest you are with yourself the more benefit this guide will be.

From there it's time to examine personal attitude and the way you look at life and the world around you. Do you have a positive or negative attitude? Do people around you like and enjoy your company or are they simply around because they have to be?

The guide will support you in identifying and confirming your real and right attitude. It will assist you in re-defining who you are and how you look at life. It will guide you through letting go of baggage from the past which has held you hostage inside your own body!

You will reignite the fires of passion and desire that burn deep within. The excitement of being alive and pursuing a dream will be yours again.

The recipe inside will stimulate your positive motivation to reach for the stars and be the person you were meant to be. A simple formula for understanding and harnessing the power of positive motivation is laid out for you step by step.

I share a frank discussion about "choices" and the responsibility we have to ourselves regarding the choices we make.

This guide is not meant to replace professional help for those that are truly struggling with life's problems. I am not a medical doctor, nor am I a psychiatrist. I am a down to earth person with a commonsense approach to living life in a way that is enjoyable and rewarding for me and the world around me. It is my hope that after reading this book, you will be enhanced by its recipe.

Notes/Ideas

Chapter One

Self Awareness

Whether it's a burning desire to reach your potential, a renewed passion for life, or a current sense of confusion and misdirection that prompts you to read this guide, welcome! You have chosen to embark on an exciting journey. There is no place more powerful than the human mind to create change. The fact that you are reading these pages suggests that you are looking for personal growth, or change in your life or both and that's exciting.

The human race is made up of optimists, pessimists and the lucky few that are half and half. I am an extreme optimist who sees the glass as half full ALL of the time. They say that the mind is like a parachute...it works best when it's open. It will be best if you can use this guide from the balanced point of view and an open mind. I suggest that you be willing to let go of some old ideas and open your mind to some new concepts. Try not to be judgmental or closed-minded in reading the ideas contained in the chapters of this guide.

My philosophy of life is to keep it simple! I approach life's issues and problems in a similar manner. We all have the tendency to complicate things in our lives which makes them appear as larger issues than they are. It's always worthwhile to take a look at things from a simple point of view. Often times, this is the clearest point of view. I believe we have to be flexible...life is not black and white, there is a lot of gray out there.

To gain maximum benefit from this book, the reader must start with a self awareness analysis. Ask yourself, where am I mentally, physically, emotionally and spiritually (MPES) in my life right now? You will be looking at where you want to be in future chapters, but for now and for a true look at yourself, you'll want to do a self analysis on the current condition of your MPES health. Before you get to that, allow me to bring up a couple of other concerns that could affect the ability to capture a true picture of your current self. Is there any unresolved "baggage" in your emotional closet?

Let's uncover it, deal with it and move forward.

First let's look at our childhood experiences and later we will consider our adult experiences.

Childhood Experiences

Childhood experiences affect us deeply. The positive experiences we remember fondly and use them constructively in our lives; however, the negative experiences traumatize and wound us severely. These we sometimes push to the back of our minds thinking we can manage them there, but they will not stay hidden forever. We need to be honest with ourselves and, if necessary, seek professional help before we can move forward.

Do an honest evaluation and if you have any negative feelings from your childhood, then NOW is the time to deal with these issues. Some people that have experienced serious childhood trauma are able to do a self analysis, come to grips and let it go while others may have misguided feelings of guilt or a lack of self esteem and often times don't really understand why. If you are one of these people, it's worth a deeper look and an investment of time.

It is indeed unfortunate that for years and years a large percentage of children have experienced trauma in the form of abuse. It is generally in the form of physical, mental or sexual abuse. Many of today's adults suffer quietly as victims of such childhood trauma. The real crime is that any of these types of childhood trauma can and do affect all areas of adult health.

In some cases, just one or two visits with a qualified mental health professional can change a person's life and their attitude for the next 50 years or more. In other cases, it is not nearly that easy. I've included some information provided by Dr. Eric Smith, a noted psychologist who has worked with over 10,000 children who were victims of one type of trauma or another. Eric S.

Smith, PHD is a specialist in forensic psychology and former Chief of Psychological Services for the Clark County Juvenile Court in Las Vegas, Nevada. He has over thirty years of clinical experience in performing psychological evaluations with pediatric, adolescent, adult, and geriatric populations. He is board certified and a Diplomat with the American Board of Forensic Examiners and attained the status of Fellow with the American College of Forensic Examiners. Dr. Smith has served as an expert witness in Family, District, and Federal Courts of Law on these subjects.

During the course of interviewing Dr. Smith in the area of Post-Traumatic Stress Disorders, he stated that *"the impact and consequences from exposure to traumatic experiences will vary greatly among individuals."* Not everyone who is exposed to a traumatic event will meet the criteria for a diagnosis of Post-Traumatic Stress Disorder. *"Over the years, clinicians would identify the effects of trauma as being that of severe anxiety, depression and personality disorders. Various researchers have been able to identify more specific symptoms and dysfunctions as somatization, dissociative responses, sexual disorders, eating disorders, difficulties with anger and aggression, substance abuse, suicidal behavior, identity disorders, amnesia, and self-mutilation."*

What is of importance to you is how any traumatic experience may have impacted upon your psychological and physical well-being. There is no question that the negative effects from stressful events could have interfered with an individual's normal course of development. The types of disorders resulting from trauma may still be interfering with the daily functioning of your role as the student, athlete, mother, father, employee, wife, husband and so on. Dr. Smith concluded by explaining that without proper assessment and treatment of post-traumatic symptomatology, the negative consequences from stressful events may result in some degree of functional impairment.

Most traumatic childhood experiences, including all types of abuse, were clearly out of the control of the child and the child (or now adult) should bear no guilt or responsibility what-so-ever for those traumatic events. So in the spirit of keeping it simple, if you feel some past trauma is causing you grief get professional help...JUST DO IT!

Adulthood Experiences

In preparing to conduct a meaningful self awareness analysis, you've got to put adult experiences in their proper place. All adult experiences fall into one of two categories. They were within our control, or they were not. The clear difference is that you cannot and should not take responsibility or have remorse for things that were out of your control. In either case it's important to recognize that the trauma is real.

Suppose your house burned down as the result of a short in an electric wire which was located inside the wall. While this has created emotional trauma, the fact that it was not your responsibility cannot be ignored and must be put in proper prospective to live a healthy life and stay in MPES balance.

What about a woman who is in an abusive relationship, or the man that is abusing his wife on a weekly or daily basis. The man has control of instigating the abuse or not and he must take the responsibility for his actions. The woman knows that the abuse is coming and is in control of whether she stays in the relationship or not and thus has a responsibility for the decision to stay! We will look at abuse in more detail in the chapter on choices, but for now let's agree that maintaining an abusive relationship is within the control of the adult.

Decision Making

Making a decision for some is easy and for others difficult. For another group, just living life each day is extremely tedious. Before you can begin to help yourself an honest self-awareness evaluation is required. There are several areas to evaluate and it's a must that you be honest with yourself. Do you make your decisions with your mind, your heart, or both?

You are exactly what and where you are supposed to be because of the decisions you've made!

A self awareness analysis requires that you are honest with yourself and are able to answer several simple questions. Answering the questions below is an exercise that should be taken very seriously. It's important to make the decision to complete the questionnaire below with sincerity. It is a confidential exercise for your personal use only.

Am I growing mentally?
(reading books, doing research, pursuing new ideas, challenging myself to become more knowledgeable) If not, why?

Am I emotionally stable?
(am I comfortable with who I am, am I contributing to my family and community, do I have love to share with those around me?) If not, why?

Am I **really** happy?
(do I like my job, do I like my spouse, am I doing any volunteer work, am I financially stable?) If not, why not?

Do I know my purpose in life?

Do I have a plan?

Do I have a vision of myself in 5 years, 10 years?

What is that vision?

STOP!

It is worthwhile to take the time to really think about the above questions and answer them. It may take a few minutes, an hour or the weekend. In any event, getting out of the pot requires a real investment of time and energy to determine where you are. The success of the exercise is indeed within your control!

Regarding your MPES health, it's not uncommon when one area slips a bit other areas follow. Sometimes you may slip into a spiral or a down cycle. The scary thing is that, it may take weeks, months or even years to figure out that you're in such a cycle. The above exercise is exactly the thing that will determine if you are and that knowledge is also the start of the new you. It is a reality check!

It could just be "the first day of the rest of your life"!

Reality Check

Although this is a brief chapter, the importance of completing the honest self-evaluation cannot be over stated. As an abstract type of thinker, it took me many years to figure out that while I had big dreams there was no possible way of getting to the destination of mental, physical, emotional, and spiritual "success" as well as financial freedom without first coming to grips with where I was at the present.

Believe me I tried to accomplish these successes many times without going through the exercise of completing a thorough self-evaluation.

In conducting workshops with thousands of people during the past fifteen years, it has become evident that skipping the self-evaluation is one of those common mistakes that we are all prone to make. When you take a moment to look at the concept with some commonsense, it becomes obvious. You must know where you are in order to determine the right path to get where you want to go.

As a part of this reality check, awareness of two different key elements comes into play. The first one is that you may not have a true sense of exactly where you want to go or which path to take. The second is the common detractor to completing the honest self-evaluation. Most of you find that where you are now is less than you had hoped for, or you perceive it as failure. In either case, many of you will go out of your way to avoid this painful knowledge and skip the self-evaluation.

Imagine for a moment that you are about to embark on a trip across country and you've decided to drive your car. If you have no real destination, a map would not be necessary as you could begin in any direction and eventually you will end up somewhere. It wouldn't really matter where you ended up since you had no destination

to begin with. Since you had no particular destination, you could not fail no matter where you
finished. You might have enjoyed the journey
and whatever the trip brought your way. It was
your decision not to make a plan and to accept
whatever came your way. That's O.K. if that is
really what you wanted.

Now imagine that you are preparing for a trip
and there are several things that you have dreamed
about seeing and experiencing. You might first
purchase a map of the entire country and then
set out to determine exactly which sights, land-
marks, theme parks and other attractions you
wish to visit. You carefully mark the various cities
or spots on the map that you intend to visit and
with that information plan the route you will
take. With the destinations now set, you'll esti-
mate, based on the time you have available, what
approximate day you would arrive at each of the
different destinations and how long you will stay
at each location. Several other details and issues
will be addressed in the planning stage including
the cost for the trip, the start date, the ending
date, contacting family or hotels to notify of your
pending arrival at their locations, etc.

The beauty of this is that the anticipation and excitement that you experience prior to the trip is rewarding and motivational in itself. You have something to look forward to as the time to depart gets closer and closer!

Now, let's get back to the self-evaluation. Looking at the different possible ways to plan a trip is a simplified example of you planning your life. One of the keys above is knowing the starting point. The map and plan could not have possibly worked if you couldn't identify on the map where you were to start with let alone where you were going.

Life is the exact same way. Neither you nor I could possibly get to our goal if we didn't have one! This is just a simple fact. If you have goals and dreams, you must identify what they are, so that you can focus on them. The route you choose to reach your goals may be different from other people, although without a roadmap to follow your chance of reaching your goal is slim at best. We will spend more time in future chapters in developing and defining the roadmaps to achieve your ultimate goals in life, but for now, it's time to focus on where you are.

Just like planning a trip, it's imperative to be able to identify the starting point. In fact, you cannot effectively begin any trip in a car or in life without having full knowledge of exactly where you are. It is only with this information as a foundation that you can possibly make plans to move forward.

I understand that some people, who may lean more to the pessimistic side, may have the opinion that all the planning in the world could be lost due to some unforeseen situation or some outside influence.

Whether the above is a planned or unplanned trip, both might experience mishaps or obstacle along the way. Either of the two could have experienced a flat tire for example. The difference is that the planned trip checked to see that the spare tire was in good shape, whereas without planning the other realized the spare was flat only when it was needed leaving them stuck on the roadway.

On any trip, there will always be unexpected or unpredictable obstacles that present themselves at the most inopportune time and it's how we deal with such events that makes up our character.

Life is the same way. It presents a variety of obstacles which provides us an opportunity to build character. The focus of this chapter is to determine what obstacles you are facing right now, what's good, what's bad, and what do you want to eliminate. With this information, you will have enough foundation to step to the next level which is deciding what you want to change and add to your life.

Take the time necessary to complete an honest self-evaluation, so that you can identify exactly where you are now.

Notes/Ideas

Chapter Two

Attitude

What is attitude and where does it come from?

From *Webster's Student Dictionary* published in 1938—attitude: 1. A person's position or bearing as showing his purpose, feeling or the like; as a threatening or kindly attitude 2. Mood, feeling, frame of mind, or the like...

Attitude is the way you look at the world. It is based on your past experiences and the way you reflect on them. When you view your past experiences in a negative way, it stands to reason your attitude may also be negative and of course when you view your past experiences as positive, it's likely reflected by a positive attitude.

One of the benefits of completing the self awareness exercise in chapter one is to gain a sense of where you are today mentally and emotionally. In the analysis of "attitude" and the cycle below, a clear understanding of your current "self" is very important. Your current self is the "result" of the decisions you've been making and those results are a part of what makes up your experiences.

If you are one of those that are truly at a point in your life where you are content with your Mental, Physical, Emotional and Spiritual (MPES) health, then you may have, even without realizing it, put yourself in positive sync within the attitude cycle below. Be clear that the cycle exists whether you have a positive or a negative attitude.

Understanding the cycle is beneficial to initiating change.

Let's take a look at the cycle which is responsible for our attitude.

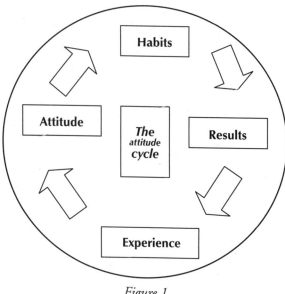

Figure 1

Habits create results, results equal experiences and those experiences are the basis for the way we look at the world. The way we look at the world equates to our attitude and our attitude creates our habits...and thus the cycle begins again.

In attempting to gain a good, healthy, positive attitude you start by looking at past experiences. You can't change your past experiences, but you can change the way you look at them. Most of adult experiences are a result of your own actions and fall somewhere within the attitude cycle above. When you are truly in search of change, the challenge is to step in and break the cycle.

When a person continues to do the same thing day after day and expects a different result... That would be insane yet...we are all guilty at some time of doing just this. Certainly, logic tells us that if we continue to do the same thing every day, we will pretty much get the same result. The problem comes when we understand this theory and yet continue to do it, looking for different results.

How do you instigate a different result? Let's analyze this by going backwards.

First, can you change your past experiences? No, although over time, you can change the way you look at those experiences and can alter the emotional feelings attached to them. Understanding this concept is very important and utilizing this technique can be the catalyst to creating a future that you never before dreamed of!

Second, can you change your daily results? Yes, albeit not by continuing to do the same things that you've been doing everyday.

Next, can you change your habits? Yes... although thought of as a difficult task, this may be the easiest part of the cycle to change.

Lastly, can you change your attitude? Yes...It requires an open mind, a sincere desire, some new habits and a dash of passion!

Based on figure #1 and the fact that the easiest part of the wheel to effect a change is habit, let's focus on habit for a bit. Some of us are addicted to our habits. I thought it would be worthwhile to simply address a couple of the most common habits. I chose these two because almost every family in America is close to someone experiencing one or both of these. Although you may not personally have one of these habits, the lessons are the same.

Alcoholism and Drug Addiction

Like the frog in the pot of cool water, unaware of his fate and the fact that he is about to die, many people are also unaware that they are in any trouble whatsoever.

Often, those suffering from an alcohol addiction don't have any idea that they are addicted. If that is a reality, they also don't realize that it is adversely affecting their daily lives, their decision making, their work production, their career and their personal relationships. Alcohol is a sneaky drug for several reasons. It is acceptable in our society and its long term adverse effects are often times difficult to see until someone's mental or physical health is affected.

Because it is so widely accepted and because it is difficult to recognize when addiction sets in, the denial factor is huge in alcoholism. George E. Vaillant, MD and a trustee of the A.A. (Alcoholic's anonymous) General Service Board has said, "The denial associated with alcoholism is cunning, baffling, and powerful and affects the patient, helper, and the community."

So let's acknowledge that alcoholism is an addiction and it also qualifies as a habit for the purposes of this guide.

The second big habit is drug addiction whether it is by choice or not. Some people are addicted to drugs because they chose to take them and became addicted while others, unfortunately, are addicted because their own medical condition called for an addictive drug to be administered and they became addicted.

In either event, the addiction is a habit that is contributing to the results which have an effect on their daily lives. You've got to take an honest look at yourself and determine if you have a problem. If you do, there is no reason to be ashamed; it is simply one of the habits that you wish to change. If it is a struggle, and it most likely will be, get the help and the support you need!

P.S. If you are a smoker, you can group yourself with the above as you are addicted to one of the most powerful drugs on earth.

I have found that with a sincere desire a logical plan can be set in place to change one's habits. When you successfully change your habits the results will change and when the results change the experience is different. This has an effect on your attitude. The CHANGE has begun.

Just because you have a formula to break the habit doesn't mean that it's easy. This will require desire and commitment. In other words—work! However with sincere desire and a plan, you can achieve anything you set your mind to do!

You must have the desire to change. It is important to put a logical plan together to change habits when the want and desire are strong enough and a real commitment is made. Many of us possess desire and yet are unable to convert that desire to the action necessary to stimulate change.

The ability to take action on desires is a major key in the change cycle!

An example of implementing change within the cycle: The Cigarette smoker:

History: You have smoked for 40 years

Situation: You experience many colds each year, bronchitis, shortness of breath, cannot take walks with grandchildren, smokers cough, hair and clothing smell of tobacco and many other concerns.

Want and desire: You have a sincere desire to quit the addiction and a willingness to commit.

Taking action: You call and set an appointment with the doctor to establish a recommended plan of action.

You have a strong "desire" and listen to the doctor.

You make the commitment; a date is set to begin your life as a non-smoker. The doctor may provide you with an audio tape to reinforce the decision along with some written materials and brochures which act as support data for you and provides additional knowledge and information about the consequences of smoking.

You are now armed with more information and knowledge and with a strong desire to quit you are motivated to the required action of not smoking. You must stay focused on the positive things that will result because of not smoking and also review the negative things that will happen if the smoking continues.

Within varying amounts of time, the effects of smoking begin to fade and benefits are revealed including a huge burst of confidence and self esteem. In just two weeks, your friends are saying how good your skin looks and asking what you're doing. This instills additional confidence and rekindles the motivational flame to keep it up. Your attitude is much more positive, your daily health is much better and you no longer smell like tobacco. However the best thing is that you are in control of your life and you are not being controlled by a cigarette. You broke the cycle with a sincere desire and a change in habit and it has an effect on everything including adding years to your life.

In this example, the smoker met with a doctor and utilized modern techniques to assist in the elimination of the addiction. While this may not work for everyone, the point is to find out what will work for you, get help if necessary and just do it. The key here is the sincere desire and the commitment to take action on it!

This chapter is about attitude and affecting change in attitude. What we have seen so far regarding the attitude cycle is that **the easiest way to affect and/or change your attitude on a permanent basis is by changing your habits. As hard as it may be to change habits, it's still the easiest way to create long term change. The strongest tool in changing a habit is the influx of a positive motivation!**

Within the "Attitude Cycle," we have focused on habits because a change in habit acts as a catalyst to effect a complete cycle change.

Let's take a look at the rest of the cycle with the "keep it simple" philosophy. Once habits change, it changes the results in that specific area. When results are different, take the time to reflect on them and pat yourself on the back for creating change. Part of creating change is the acceptance of responsibility for your life including all that you do and the results you achieve. Plain and simple, it's all up to you.

Can you change results without changing a habit?

All that you get in life is a "result" of what you do. The question is, is everything you do a habit? The answer is no. Because not everything you do is a habit, it means that you can change results by simply doing different things. You are not forced to necessarily break or change a habit to change results.

I'd like to relate a story to you about a family friend of many years.

He is considered a financially successful man. Over the years, I have had occasion to introduce him to many different people. Often times the first several comments out of his mouth are condescending and sarcastic in what he believes is a fun or funny kind of way. In many cases, the people that I have introduced him to will come to me later and say, "Wow, he's a jerk."

In some cases, if a longer term relationship develops between our family friend and the new people, they come to like him as they get to know him better; however, in many cases they continue to believe he is a jerk. Personally, I believe, for whatever reason, he has created a "habit" of being condescending and sarcastic to people in general...and...the result is that people don't like him.

I believe if he was to be more sincere, he'd be happier and the people around him would have much more respect for him. I also believe it would have an effect on his business relationships. His employees would respect him more and work harder for him if he simply treated them better.

I don't believe our family friend has a clue. The observation is that while we may not look at personality traits and different characteristics of an individual as habits many of them are just that, habits.

The point is this; whether his actions are a habit or not, the results are a direct response to his actions. If he were to do different things the effective results would be different. This is simple and it's the same as saying, if you don't act like a jerk, no one will know that you are a jerk.

It reminds me of the old saying: "It's better to remain silent and be thought a fool than to speak and remove all doubt." In some cases, we all say things that shouldn't be said. It took lots of work for me to learn to keep my mouth shut when there is no benefit in opening it!

We all have the ability to create the results we are looking for with a sincere desire, an established well thought out plan and ultimately by taking the action necessary to move towards that desire.

When I was 14 years old, I worked in the town's primary coffee shop where I grew up. One day, one of the two owners, Joe, pulled me aside and told me it was time that I learned how to operate the cash register, so that I could check customers out as they stood at the register to pay.

He said that there were three rules that I **must** follow every single time:

Rule # 1: NEVER... EVER make someone wait to pay. Get to them immediately.

Rule # 2: ALWAYS SMILE...even if you are not happy.

Rule # 3: ALWAYS SAY..." Thank you very much...we'll see you again soon."

As we discussed the rules in more detail as a fourteen year old boy might want to do, Joe explained that the customer should never have to wait to pay. "It irritates them," he said, "to have to wait in a line to give their money to someone. When it's time for them to leave and they want to go...be there...DON'T MAKE THEM WAIT"!

Joe went on in a stern and serious voice..."I don't care if you don't like the customer and I don't care if you're not happy that particular day, just make sure you are smiling." He explained to me that the smile was very important, that each and every person that was giving us money was our boss, and if it weren't for them and their money, I wouldn't have a job and the restaurant wouldn't be open. The "thank you" and the "we'll see you again soon" was a personal touch to let the customer know we cared about them!

While I never really gave much thought to Joe's well thought out plan, it's very clear to me today just how effective his plan was. This little restaurant was by far, the busiest restaurant in the city for my entire childhood. Joe and his partner, Pat, had a plan which was geared to the results we call success!

Results are experience!

In looking at the "attitude" cycle in figure # 1, we see that experiences are located in the circle as the next item influencing and mostly responsible for our attitude. The experiences we have been through are largely responsible for the way we look at life.

If we have success in our personal and business lives chances are that we have a pretty good attitude. If we are experiencing a hostile workplace our attitude about work is probably not so good. If we are experiencing turbulence in our personal and love life, there is a good chance that our attitude regarding our personal lives and loved ones is less than stellar.

If we are really attempting to stimulate change the key to looking at the experience portion of the cycle is to understand that they are what they are.... More important than that part of the cycle is the positive we can take from it.

All experiences can have a positive message.

I'd like to share a personal experience about my life and relate the effect I believe it has had on my attitude for the past 35 plus years.

My father died in 1957 when I was four years old. It was unfortunate as he had a staphylococcus infection in his blood and the only commonly used antibiotic in 1957 was penicillin. The problem was that he was allergic to penicillin and he died. I vaguely remember my mother driving us to the hospital almost every day to go see Daddy. I remember that the nurses would put a foot stool next to my Dad's bed so that I could stand on it and see and talk to my Dad. I remember saying to him, "Don't worry Daddy, God will take care of you."

At the age of four, I hardly knew my Dad and was very sad when my Mom explained that he had gone to heaven. I had two older sisters that were six and seven at the time. My Dad was thirty-one when he died. My mother has never remarried. I know that what happened was the same for all of us although the way we looked at it and how it impacted our lives may have been different for each of us.

Some years later, in 1971, while dealing with a medical issue called Bell's Palsy, I was able to reflect on my father's death in a different light than I had ever imagined before. While the left side of my face had become 100% paralyzed and the doctors had performed surgery, they advised that I may never get any movement back.

They were able to tell me about a month later that the surgery was unsuccessful and unless the nerves grew back on their own, the paralysis would be permanent. They said if that were the case, they could perform plastic surgery to install implants in my face to hold it up.

All of this information was quite disturbing, especially for a 19-year-old boy. With various thoughts of a major life change, looking like a freak, slobbering out of the left side of my mouth all day, not able to speak properly as the left side of my mouth would not move, not able to hold food in my mouth and having to manually open and close my left eye with the use of my hand, life had suddenly become a major bummer!

It was then, while reflecting, that I thought of my Father and his untimely death. I thought about the fact that he was unable to see his kids grow up, not able to play baseball with his son, not able to take his daughters to the Father/ Daughter Dinner Dance, never able to love his wife again. It was then that a new reality came to me...paralysis of the left side of my face for life...HA! No big deal! I recognized that being alive was the ultimate gift. That's when I came to the conclusion that the paralysis was no big deal, in fact not very many things are a big deal!

I was learning from a past experience a whole new appreciation for life. There have been other times in my life when I have called on these memories and reflected on my new attitude about life. It's as though there is a calm and clear understanding in my being that reminds me, even when in a down cycle, that being alive is like having a new opportunity every single day to start over.

It's what I lean on to rejuvenate my attitude. What is the pleasant, positive, or otherwise powerful emotions that you have tied to a past experience that helps you stay positive?

Sometimes the positive message of a past experience does not jump out at you and say, "Here I am." It is worthwhile to take the time and identify several past experiences that you have tied to positive emotional feelings.

Don't be Fooled by the Short Term Fix!

From time to time, we all either attend a motivational program, or we watch a television show, or a movie that has some motivational value. Sometimes, as a result of the brief experience, we say to ourselves, "that's it, I'm changing my life." It's not bad when that happens; however, more times than not, it is short lived unless steps are taken to change habits and actions which in turn effect a long term change.

Rudolph Giuliani, perhaps the greatest mayor that New York City has ever seen, had this to say about leadership and change: "Inspiration must be taken whenever and wherever it comes and sources of strength appear in unexpected places."

The absolute best time to commit to a plan of long term change is when you have just been motivated or uplifted in some way, whether by a speaker, a movie, a friend, or situation. It is at these exact times that having a plan for review or making a plan is in the best interest of change. It is at these times, as brief as they may be, that you come face to face with the knowledge that you are in a pot of water about to boil. It is a powerful time when we can face personal knowledge of a life changing magnitude. We have a responsibility to ourselves to act on it.

Are you going to do something with this knowledge, awareness, or motivation? Or...will you simply let it slip away and lose yet another opportunity to initiate change in your life.

Ideas About the Cycle

Until you have looked at and studied the cycle, you may not have ever considered why or where a bad mood or a down attitude came from. An understanding of the attitude cycle makes it easy for me to do two very important things to constantly move forward.

1. It provides me the opportunity to laugh at myself when I find myself getting frustrated, angry, or otherwise emotionally out of control.

2. Understanding the cycle allows me to easily do a self analysis, determine where I've made a wrong turn and then get my attitude back on track.

Like anything new, it takes a bit of reflection and work on a daily basis to change or improve an attitude.

If I were to focus on any one key about attitude, it would be this reality: How you look at things and how you feel and react to things around you is strictly up to you. It is within your power and will to act and react in any way you want to. It's all up to you!

Attitude Summary

Since the formula indicates that our attitude, in large part, is based on our habits and our experiences, it's time to take a closer look at what is motivating us to do certain things, whether habit or not.

The first step in changing things requires a review of what you are doing and then the decision of "do I even want to change?" Most of us want to change and grow in some areas and we even have some strong desire for change. The common stumbling block is the inability to take action towards initiating the change!

If you are looking to improve your attitude and have a desire to initiate change in your life, you are on the right track. This guide will assist you in laying the foundation for change. You now understand why you possess the attitude you have and the initial steps needed to modify your attitude.

The next chapter will start you on an exciting journey of change. It will provide you with the power to "UNLOCK THE MOTIVATION WITHIN."

Notes/Ideas

Chapter 3

Unlocking the Motivation Within

The key to unlocking motivation has been the foundation for many books. In this chapter, we will focus on the steps and truths necessary to open the motivation vault and pump life back into dreams that have become stale.

At first glance, motivation may seem like a concept because not everyone appears to have it. It would be great if we could turn it on like an electric light, flip the switch to the up position and BINGO...you're totally motivated.

Past experience has taught me that the deeper we are in a down cycle the harder it is to get motivated in the right direction. I find this ironic because these are the times that motivation is needed to get ourselves to a new place mentally and emotionally.

One of the areas that I often speak of in my programs around the country is Mental, Physical, Emotional and Spiritual health (MPES). Most of us tend to make life and our MPES health more complicated than it is. The switch to turn on motivation is slightly different in each of us and is less complex than once thought.

A Look at Drugs and Motivation

Many people are on drugs today to treat apathy, depression or some other "motivational" related defect. The drug companies have been able to convince many of us that drugs will balance our lives and make everything OK again. Unfortunately, in some cases, the medical profession has contributed to the demise of MPES health in many people.

I am not suggesting that the entire medical profession is involved in a conspiracy, I'm simply stating that drug use is out of control.

We all get depressed from time to time and that's normal. Some situations require the use of drugs to provide medical stability in people's lives. However, many of us have erroneously bought into well thought-out advertising campaigns by the pharmaceutical industry and look for a drug to somehow equalize and bring us into balance for every weakness and conceivable ailment.

The point here is this: We have got to step up and take more responsibility for our lives...PERIOD. Sometimes it takes work to figure out what's wrong. It takes some thought. It requires honesty with yourself and a true desire to move from one level to another. It would be wonderful if we could flip a switch or take a pill and have instant motivation; however that's not reality.

Getting Motivated!

I learned a trick in 1982 from a man named Paul. He was my Dale Carnegie Sales Course instructor. I believe it was a part of the regular course materials and it was powerful. It still works today. You may find this to be a ridiculous exercise and that's OK... Give it a try!

Stand up and say with some excitement in your voice:

"Act enthusiastic and you'll be enthusiastic, act enthusiastic and you'll be enthusiastic, act enthusiastic and you'll be enthusiastic."

Although this is not a study guide in neuro-linguistics, there are a couple of simple elements in the brain arena that make perfect sense. This is one of them: When the brain hears something, it does not distinguish whether it is true or not, it simply processes the information as reality. The following is an example.

You are sound asleep in the comfort of your own bed at home. It is a windy, cold night and appears that it's going to rain. You've been asleep for about three hours when you wake to someone trying to get in the front door...you sit up...you listen and yes, someone is turning the door handle and it sounds like they are committed to getting into the house.

The sound stops for a moment and through a window you clearly see the shadows of what looks like two large men walking around the house. Fear has set in and you think...I've got to call the police...just as you question whether you should do that... you hear a loud cracking sound at the front door. It sounds like they are attempting to kick the door down. You are now convinced that the front door is coming down and you are in great danger. Your body is flushed with adrenaline and you are emotionally charged and now a bit frantic mentally.

WAIT!

The truth of the situation is this: A small branch from a nearby tree had been broken off by the wind and had worked its way to your front door where the wind was hitting the branch just right so that it sounded like someone banging on the front door....The shadows were just shadows that you thought looked like two men, it was simply the light of the moon through the clouds shining through the trees and bushes that generated the body images. While there was nothing wrong or really bad happening, our body was reacting in a way that it believed something was really wrong, the adrenaline was pumping and our minds were racing, this was for just a minute or two "our reality." This is our brain and body reacting to something it thinks is true.

"Act enthusiastic and you'll be enthusiastic" as silly as that may sound is a real start toward making a change in the way we feed our brain and operate on a daily basis. Some of us need more help than others in creating a positive attitude which makes stimulating positive motivation a lot easier. It is far easier to turn on the motivation switch when we have a positive attitude. Putting a big smile on your face and doing the enthusiastic exercise in front of a mirror will stimulate the positive senses in your brain. Done daily, with gusto, will create a positive attitude!

Commonsense suggests that attitude and motivation have something to do with one another. Based on the attitude circle and the impact of habits, wouldn't it be nice if you had the **motivation** to change a habit?

What if it were a habit to look into the mirror at yourself each morning and say "I am a winner," "People like to be around me," "I am very successful in personal and business affairs," "I am efficient with my time in a very pleasant way," "I am a winner," "I am focused," "I am powerful," "I am a winner." This is one form of self talk that can have a powerful influence on your attitude especially when it's based on a sincere desire to foster change and growth.

Let's be clear on this. If there is no sincere desire to change and no commitment to change, the exercise above will have minimal value. In order to determine the desire and commitment level, a good idea is to conduct a motivation check.

Motivation Check!

Here is a question to ask yourself— Am I motivated?

There are probably several different ways to check the level or degree of one's motivation. This may be a difficult question for many of us. I believe that the more difficult the question is to answer the more we lack positive motivation.

I sometimes run late to the office or occasionally to a meeting. My loving wife is quick to point out to me that I have never been late for a tee time (golf game). Apparently my motivation to be on time for a golf game far outweighs my motivation for being on time to the office.

I'm not sure if that's a clear way to measure motivation level however, whenever I am excited about doing something, it always seems easier to get up in the morning and get going.

Wouldn't it be nice if we were all that excited about getting out of bed every day just to get our day started? Well, some people are that motivated about getting up and starting the day, every day. Some people recognize and appreciate the fact that they are alive and have the "opportunity" to get up and live life today and are grateful for it! Others, that may be taking life for granted, in a sad state or out of balance in their MPES health, don't seem to be as motivated or excited about bouncing up and getting the day started.

Let's take a moment and look at the word motive: **Motive: that which incites to action; inner impulse; dominant theme.**

The key in the definition is that "motivation" is responsible for what incites us to action, it is the reason for the action we take and it's based on our inner impulse. We all take some sort of action each and every day.

Motivation Truth number 1: We are all moti- vated! Motivation is the reason that we do what we do. It is the EXACT reason that we take a particular action. The benefit of this truth is the understanding that we all have motivation so there is no need to find it. It may just require that we re-direct it to cause a more positive action!

Based on this meaning, the question of "are we motivated?" certainly comes right back to what our inner impulse is or what our dominant theme is in life. Are you aware of your inner pulse and what it's saying to you? Did you even know you have a "dominant theme?"

We must spend some time here on this reality because this is directing the actions we are taking every day.

I'll bet if you asked a really close friend to give some thought to it and tell you what they saw your dominant theme as being, they'd share an answer with you that may not be how you see yourself at all.

In a sincere effort to refocus ourselves on our inner impulse and dominant theme I have bor- rowed the "getting started" Motivational checklist from Jason Gracia and included it below. I suggest that adequate time be given to this exercise and that the written results be placed into your new idea notebook or a personal log or diary of some sort. Taking the time to complete the checklist and recording the information where you can access it and see it every day is truly the beginning of major change. It will clarify your dominant theme, direction and motivation and move you six months to a year ahead in just a few days.

Motivation Checklist—Getting Started

Before any improvements can be made in your life, you have to know what you want. Use the questions below as a jumpstart to getting clear about what it is you desire for your future.

❑ What are you physical goals? What is your ideal weight? Ideal diet? Ideal exercise plan? Take time this month to discover what you want physically.

❑ How much money do you want to make? How much in savings? How much invested? Take time this month to discover what you want financially.

❑ What kind of relationships do you want to have with others? What friendships do you need to strengthen? How can you better care for your spouse? Take time this month to discover what you want out of your relationships.

❑ What new skills do you want to learn? What talents would you like to possess? Take time this month to discover what new skills and abilities you would like to learn.

❑ What improvements do you want to make in your career? Do you want a new job? A promotion? A change in responsibility? Take time this month to discover what you want in your career.

by Jason Michael Gracia—Motivation123
Get your FREE Motivation123 Idea-Kit filled with ideas and techniques to help you create lasting change and enjoy greater happiness and success at the Motivation123 Web site. www.motivation123.com.

As simple as the previous check list is, it is surprising how many people do not have any clear vision of what they truly want and where they are going!

Some of us are so busy with "life" that we are unable to clearly identify what we represent.

The above check list can be used to clarify what it is that you really desire.

Many people are hard pressed to verbalize what they desire in life and often times their comments may end with "I'm not sure what I want." It is extremely rewarding to be able to identify your own personal desire in life!

Motivation Truth number 2: Sincere desire is the key and the first stepping stone to creating more "positive" motivation in your life. This desire must come from within your self, be positive and be based in reality.

It is important that the desire you have be your personal desire. You should not feel pressure to do something to satisfy someone else's picture of who you are and/or what they believe you should do. The desire you embrace must be based on your genuine and personal feelings. Early in this chapter I said that the switch to turn on motivation is slightly different in each of us and this is the reason. It's based on different desires. While some people share some similar desires, there can be as many different desires as there are people.

Believe it or not, most people are involved in pursuing goals and desires that were placed on them by society, their family or another outside source other than themselves.

This again is where the motivation check list can and will be quite useful if the proper time and personal soul searching is employed to answer the questions. In evaluating yourself, stop to ask the question; "is this my real desire or am I making decisions based on what I believe is expected of me by someone else?" ...or...has society or peer pressure made me feel that... "this is the right thing for me to do" or "to be responsible, I must do these things." Family and society expectations that are poured upon us from the time we are very young can easily be confused as our own desires!

Think about how many people are working in jobs they hate. Many of them are in dead end jobs making just enough money to get to their next check. They complain about it daily and yet continue to go back to work on the same job year in and year out...why?

Somewhere along the line they came to believe that they had a responsibility to do so to provide for their family or they believe that's all they know how to do. For what ever the reason, they are not motivated to do something else that they might love. In most cases people are acting on some perceived expectations rather than their own desires. The truth is that they are settling for a life less than the dreams they once had!

It may feel strange to sit down and re-evaluate your self at the age of 30, 40, 50, 60, 70 or 80 and come to the possible conclusion that you might not be "being" what you want at this time! At the same time that this reality check may seem strange or weird it can be unbelievably exciting to shed old perceptions and embrace your true desires and dreams!

To this point in unlocking the motivation within, we have two truths. First we are all motivated and second desire is the key and the first stepping stone to creating "positive" motivation. The next question is where do we go from here? The answer is Motivation truth number 3:

Motivation Truth number 3: If you can conceive it and believe it, you can make it a reality!

This may sound very simple and uncomplicated. Early on in this chapter, I wrote that the switch to turn on motivation appears to be much less complicated than once thought. It's true. What we know, is that many people have had dreams to achieve certain things with the belief that they could, while others thought they were crazy and dismissed them as dreamers. Take a look at some people that were very ordinary before they became famous for certain things.

On May 5, 1954, no track star, no man, no woman, no one in history had ever run a mile in less than four minutes. In fact, the physiologists of the day suggested that it would be an extreme health hazard and that it could not be done. On May 6, 1954, Roger Bannister ran a mile in 3:59:4, under four minutes. He had dreamed about it for several years as had other track stars of the era, but on May 6, he did it...the first man in the history of the world and the only man in the history of the world to do it! 46 days later his record was broken by John Landy and by the end of 1957, 16 others had run the four minute mile, today it's fairly common. You can clearly see here that when the now "Sir" Roger Bannister ran the four minute mile he also broke the psychological barrier as well, opening the door for thousands of others to follow.

In 1800, an English scientist spent thousands of hours and failed thousands of times but ultimately invented an electric light bulb. It wasn't until 1879 that Thomas Edison and his group really perfected the electric light bulb. The point is that prior to 1800 the thought was unheard of and yet, can you imagine the world today without the electric light!

In 1902, an employee for the Buffalo Forge Company, an engineer, developed the air conditioner. His name was Willis H. Carrier. This young man went on to open the Carrier Corporation.

In 1972 a 28 year old man by the name of Noland Bushnell invented the first video game, Pong. He later went on to found a little company called "Atari".

In 1898 a baby was born in what was then Kiev, Russia by the name of Golda Mabovitch (Meir). She and her family immigrated to the United States when she was a child. In 1921, now a young lady and married she began a life of public service when she and her husband moved to Palestine. Golda Meir was loved by her people and well respected by the Arab nations and the world. She served as the Prime Minister of Israel from 1969 to 1974. She remains the definition of greatness to many people the world over.

Between 1973 and 1975, a young man from Seattle had a vision that a personal computer would be of value to every person and should be in every home and should be very affordable. In 1975, he dropped out of Harvard University and opened a little company called Microsoft. He hooked up with his childhood friend, Paul Allen. His name was Bill Gates and he is now a billionaire. Bill Gates and his wife Melinda have endowed a foundation in the amount of $24 billion to support philanthropic initiatives in the areas of global health and learning, with the hope that as we move into the 21st century, advances in these critical areas will be available for all people. They have additionally funded untold other charities with billions of dollars.

Whether we are talking about Bill Gates, the Wright brothers or Golda Meir, they are just like you and I. What we know about these folks now is that they all had sincere desire and the ability to dream. They all had the ability to conceive and believe in their personal desires and were able to stay focused on those dreams and desires for the long term. All of them took baby steps to start with. The Wright brothers with bicycles, Bill Gates working out of his garage and Golda Meir's family emigrating to the United States because they were poor and starving in Russia.

Desires and dreams are a lot like goals. Some years ago, I was told that the Harvard Business School did a survey of their top and most successful graduates to determine what they had in common and in an effort to find their common denominator. Those surveyed were now the CEOs and presidents of small and large Fortune 500 companies. The one single commonality was that all had goals that were written down and goals that they reviewed on a regular basis. They in essence, reduced their dreams and desires for achievement to written goals on paper and kept those in front of them to maintain focus.

If the want and desire are real and it's a sincere goal based in reality, there is no reason why you cannot make it happen. The beauty of the motivation check list, if used properly, is that it will clarify what your real and sincere desires are! Again and at the risk of being repetitive, it's imperative that you are crystal clear on your true desires. If you are creating goals that are not real, not yours or not sincere you will invest time, energy and enthusiasm in them for the short term but they cannot possibly stand up under the test of time. Life is too short to attempt to live the wrong dream.

Just like the people above that became famous for their contributions to their communities and the world, there are thousands of others with stories and lives that are just as exciting. You probably know of someone in your own life that has influenced you in an extraordinary way. It could be an immediate family member, relative, friend or teacher that had a big impact on your life. It could have been the coach you had or someone you grew up with. It could have been a professor, priest or rabbi or any number of other people in your life.

We are all born with greatness inside of us. We all have an influence on others. We all are extraordinary people.

Back to motivation truth number 3:

If you can conceive it and believe it, you can make it a reality!

Although you can conceive and believe in a concept, idea or dream and you have the opportunity to make it a reality it will require a strong buy-in to motivation truth number 4.

Motivation Truth number 4: The only proof that true motivation exists is by the ACTION that demonstrates it! Without action, motivation is a meaningless thought.

I've attached parts of an article which I wrote some time ago for *Success Magazine* which is published in Las Vegas, Nevada.

Are You Motivated?

Many times I've had students and co-workers ask me where I get my energy from or how come I am so motivated? I have given much thought to this question and a little research and this is what I've come up with.

First I went to the Encyclopedia Britannica *and looked up "motivation". This is what it said.* **Factors within a human being or animal that arouse and direct goal-orientated behavior.**

Next I researched some of the great and respected minds of modern times on the subject. Many of the early researchers, influenced by Charles Darwin, ascribed much "motivational type" behavior to instinct. Mr. Freud bottom lined our motives as those behaviors which stemmed from irrational instinctive urges or from our subconscious.

Cognitive psychologists have found that a motive sensitizes a person to information relating to that motive: a hungry subject, for example, will perceive food stimuli as larger than other stimuli and will thus do what is necessary to obtain food.

Finally, I interviewed several really successful real estate agents. Each of the agents I interviewed made more than a million dollars in income last year. The interviews were conducted separately. I asked each of them several questions. Where does your motivation come from? How do you stay motivated? Do you lose your motivation some times? And lastly I asked them what must a person do to become successful?

Here is a synopsis of their answers:

All were able to relate to something in their upbringing that they relied upon for the beginnings of their personal motivation and drive. Some relied on what they perceived as positive experiences while others clearly reflected on negative experiences. In any event, they all agreed that their current motivation was based on the way they looked at their life and work today.

Regarding the question of staying motivated, all of those interviewed agreed that it was their way of life to keep themselves motivated. e.g.: Listen to motivational tapes, reading books, attending seminars and self talk. All agreed that they liked being a motivated person and that it made life more enjoyable for them. In fact, they couldn't imagine not being a motivated person.

Loss of motivation: All acknowledged that "stuff" happens to everyone from time to time that affects their motivation level. All seemed to have a plan ready for when that took place, surround themselves with positive input.

The last question I asked was the "what must a person do to become successful" question. They all said that it requires action! In their separate ways, each suggested that a person must have a plan and/or at least know where they want to go and then **TAKE ACTION** towards achieving the goals.

Based on the interviews I conducted and my personal belief about motivation and its origins, I would say this: all people are motivated in one way or another. Some people are motivated to do great things and live their dream, some to reach for the stars as if there were no limits and others are motivated to do nothing! (often referred to as a lack of motivation.)

Energy and motivation come from within and require some sort of action to get them started. When we can utilize external stimuli in addition to some personal desire and get excited about something...we have a winning formula for motivation. As we take action, we've got to keep in mind that most results will not be immediate and that's o.k. Stay in the game and have a healthy understanding that evidence of motivation and change may appear slowly.

Life is too short not to be excited about it. Put yourself in a position or situation everyday to get excited or motivated! Surround yourself with successful minded people and get reconnected to positive energy through tapes, CDs and books. Nobody but you is going to make your dreams come true and nobody but you *is going to take the initiative to stimulate your personal motivation. There is no magic pill!*

It turns out that different things motivate different people. In answer to the original question above, "What motivates me?" Here is the answer: I love to travel and play golf abroad, I love fine dining and a good wine and I love spending time with my wife, family and those that I care about. The END.

The point of Motivation Truth number 4 and the article is this. It would be unrealistic to believe that just thinking of something will make it happen. Are you a person who has a desire to do something but has yet to take action on it? Do you find that you are telling yourself or others of your desire to get a new job, travel somewhere, buy a new car, increase your sales, get a promotion or achieve some other goal and yet you have taken no action to even begin that possibility.

Let's be clear that all goals and dreams start with thought so having the thought or idea is a good thing. Having a thought and NOT acting on it with action is what makes a dream, just that, a dream and nothing more! With no action, it will begin to become a negative resource as a meaningless and powerless thought in your mind-set which will distract you from accomplishing meaningful things. The reason behind this is simple, the longer we cling to an idea and do nothing to grow or initiate its reality, the more our psyche acknowledges that we don't have the ability to accomplish it! This is where the "fear of failure" factor grows stronger in our minds whether we realize it or not.

The reason we are not actively pursuing the dream is that we have not convinced ourselves that it is possible to turn the dream into reality or the thought that we may fail is causing a greater level of resistance than the sweetness associated with the success.

Most people will not attempt something because the fear of failure or the pain associated with invest-ing time, energy and money into something and not accomplishing it, exceeds the benefits associated with the success of the project. The pain associ-ated with failure is stronger than the benefits and pleasure associated with the success. This means that the sincere desire is stronger to avoid the pain than it is to achieve the goal! As long as that is where the sincere desire is...no meaningful action will be taken to accomplish the long term goal.

You now understand exactly what prevents a desire to take on the action necessary so that it can become a reality. It is that YOU are not convinced to pursue the goal for the risk of not achieving it!

Allow me to take you back to a point in time when your thought was pure and based in nothing but truth! When you were considered a pioneer, when you were filled with passion and commitment and when nothing could stop you from pursuing your goals.

You were between three and twenty-four months old when you made a conscious decision that you wanted to walk. From the very beginning there were obstacles to overcome. First, you couldn't even stand up let alone walk and second, this balancing thing on two legs was quite a trick. Even though you wanted to walk like the big people, you recognized that you'd have to start with what they called crawling.

It seemed like a lot of work, putting one knee in front of the other without collapsing on your tummy. After establishing a little balance fairly

Chapter 3 Unlocking the Motivation Within   79

close to the floor, you were ready to begin the standing phase. Fortunately, there were chairs, cribs, couches and people to utilize in the standing process. You fell on your butt quite a bit and sometimes on your face, but you were relentless in your pursuit and could not be stopped. It really didn't matter what anyone said to you, you were committed and you worked on it every day, almost to the point that you were obsessed with the idea of walking.

It was no longer a matter of **if** you would walk, if was clearly a matter of **when**. The closer you sensed that you were to reaching your goal, the more excited you were about achieving it and the harder you worked at accomplishing it! Finally, you stood and you walked!

Your family cheered and applauded wildly shouting words of encouragement and there you stood with a smile on your face and a sense of total accomplishment.

Commitment is Essential!

As we grow older, we learn many things about ourselves, the world and life in general. We begin to incorporate rationale and justification as a part of our reasoning to do or not to do certain things. This is way more complicated than the process we used above when focused on the goal of walking. It's easy to talk ourselves out of things when we are not truly committed to them. If we are not truly committed to an idea, dream or desire and yet we want to be...it will require additional information and knowledge about the long term benefits of the dream. You have an obligation to yourself to do the research and provide yourself with the knowledge and information necessary to make a decision that you are committed and take action to achieve it, or decide against the idea because it's not really a sincere desire and let it go.

Either of the decisions is fine as long as it is based in truth and sincerity. With respect to the soul searching that takes place in determining if something is really a sincere desire or not, remember, Motivation Truth number 4: The only proof that true motivation exists is by the ACTION that demonstrates it! Without action, motivation is a meaningless thought.

Before we list the last motivation truth, let's quickly look at the first four:

1. Everybody is motivated....

2. Sincere desire is the stepping stone, its key!

3. If we can conceive it and believe it we can make it reality.

4. We MUST take action to achieve it.

Lastly, we must have commitment with integrity. This term is used to describe that the commitment must be based in "goodness". It must be for the right reasons and based in truth and in harmony with your spiritual self.

Motivation Truth number 5: Commitment with integrity will overcome all obstacles.

"Obstacles are something that people see when they lose sight of their goals." There is nothing more powerful than true and sincere human desire. You make commitments with integrity most days of your life.

It could be something as simple as going to the movies. You speak with a friend on the phone and decide to go see a new movie. You have agreed with your friend in "good faith" to go and watch the movie together. This in itself is a simple commitment with integrity and the discussion with your friend was an action which brought you closer to the goal.

As you approach the ticket window and actually purchase the tickets, you are taking another action as well as making a financial commitment to attend the showing. Because the tickets are only good for that day or evening, you risk the loss of the investment should you change your mind and leave prior to the movie. Lastly, you and your friend enter the theater, give your tickets to the usher, find your seats and watch the movie!

This is a simple example of "commitment with integrity." As you break it down, you can see all five of the motivation truths.

1. You and your friend were motivated to see the movie.

2. The sincere desire was acted on by the initial discussion with your friend about the want to go see the movie.

3. Once the desire to see the movie was established in your own mind, you believed that you could sell your friend on the idea as well and you did with the phone call.

4. The ACTION you took was the calling your friend and then following up and physically going to the theater.

5. The commitment with integrity existed all the way through the process. You were committed even when you initiated the call to your friend, set the meeting and went to the movies. Once the desire was clear and the decision was made, doubt never entered the picture and that is "Commitment with Integrity".

The above example is a rather simplified look at commitment with integrity. While the item or thing or action that you are committing to may be grand in scope such as obtaining a college degree, learning how to play the piano, getting a promotion or changing your career altogether, it is always best to keep the commitment "simple" and straight forward. In other words, once you have made the decision to go forward and commit, the achievement of the goal becomes almost automatic.

*"Always bear in mind, that
your own resolution to succeed
is more important than any other thing."*
—Abraham Lincoln

Some Keys to Remember

Unlocking the motivation within will require different levels of attention for different people. Some things will be harder for you and some things will be easier for you. A few helpful keys are listed below:

1. Do the written motivation checklist and write down what it is you really want in life.

2. Set a deadline for completing different tasks including the completion of the written motivation check list.

3. Write a plan as to when you will complete the different aspects of the wants.

4. Write down the strategies you will use to accomplish the tasks along the way. (the nuts and bolts of getting things done)

5. Understand that the more results you can see yourself, the more excitement and motivation is created to continue.

6. Even in long term goals and wants, set short term measurements to identify your achievements along the way.

Now that we have taken a look at attitude and motivation, it's time to evaluate the opportunities and choices we face each day. It's what we do day by day that makes us who we are. It's all about choice.

Notes/Ideas

Chapter 4

Choices

We all have choices to make each day. Although the choices we make may be motivated by different areas of our life, they are all our choices. Free will is a wonderful thing!

Naturally, the choices we make each day affect our position in life along with our attitude, motivation, self esteem, level of success, happiness and even those around us. Some, reading this guide, may have already slipped into the, "yea, but in my situation it's different because of this reason or that reason". This type of thinking is usually associated with those who choose to be on, what many call, "a victim trip".

Many are able to convince themselves that even though they are in a bad situation (home, relationship, work, etc.), it's not their fault. It is because of someone or something else. We may be that person, or know someone who is that person...never at fault for the situation they find themselves in.

Those that remove themselves from any responsibility for their current life's situation tend to be the same group that don't or won't take responsibility for the choices they have made in the past and are making on a daily basis.

Before we travel too far down this road, let's establish some basic human dynamics about life, death, responsibility and who gets to make all these choices.

When we wake up in the morning, who gets to decide whether our attitude will be positive or negative? We do! It's our choice. If something bad happens, the way that we react to it and allow it to influence our life is up to us, our choice. When someone comes to us complaining, we can choose to buy into their problem and get down about it, or we can focus on the positive side of life, our choice.

You might say wait a minute here, it's not that easy! You're making it sound much easier than it is in real life. I am a believer in truth and the truth is that "life is all about choices." You choose how to react to situations. You choose how people affect your mood. Your life, your choice!

These basic thoughts were relayed to me by a friend of mine named Carlos. Carlos sent me this story about choices.

Choices:

Michael is the kind of guy you love to hate. He is always in a good mood and always has something positive to say. When someone would ask him how he was doing, he would reply, "If I were any better, I'd be twins!" He was a natural motivator. If an employee was having a bad day, Michael was there telling the employee how to look on the positive side of the situation.

Seeing this style really made me curious, so one day I went up to Michael and asked him, "I don't get it! You can't be a positive person all of the time. How do you do it?"

Michael replied, "Each morning I wake up and say to myself, you have two choices today. You can choose to be in a good mood, or you can choose to be in a bad mood, I choose to be in a good mood. Each time something bad happens, I can choose to be a victim, or I can choose to learn from it, I choose to learn from it. Every time someone comes to me complaining, I can choose to accept their complaining, or I can point out the positive side of life, I choose to point out the positive side of life."

"Yeah right, it's not that easy", I protested. "Yes it is" Michael said. "Life is all about choices. When you cut away all the junk, every situation is a choice. You choose how you react to situations. You choose how people affect your mood. You choose to be in a good mood or a bad mood. The bottom line" said Michael, "it's your choice how you live your life."

I reflected on what Michael said, Carlos wrote. *Soon thereafter, I left the tower industry to start my own business. We lost touch, but I often thought about him when I made a choice about life instead of reacting to it. Several years later, I heard that Michael was involved in a serious accident, falling some sixty feet from a communication tower. After 18 hours of surgery and weeks of intensive care, Michael was released from the hospital with rods placed in his back. I saw Michael about six months after the accident. When I asked him how he was, he replied, "If I were any better, I'd be twins. Wanna see my scars?" I declined to see his wounds, but I did ask him what was going through his mind as the accident took place. "The first thing that went through my mind was the well-being of my soon to be born daughter," Michael replied. "Then as I lay on the ground, I remembered that I had two choices: I could choose to live, or I could choose to die. I chose to live." "Weren't you scared? Did you loose consciousness?" I asked. Michael continued, "...the paramedics were great. They kept telling me I was going to be fine. But when they wheeled me into the ER and I saw the expressions on the face of the doctors and nurses, I got really scared. In their eyes, I read 'he's a dead man'. I knew I needed to take action."*

"What did you do?" I asked. "Well, there was a big burly nurse shouting questions at me," said Michael. "She asked if I was allergic to anything. Yes, I replied." The doctors and nurses stopped working as they waited for my reply. I took a deep breath and yelled, "Gravity." Over their laughter, I told them, "I am choosing to live. Operate on me as if I am alive, not dead." Michael lived, thanks to the skill of his doctors, but also because of his amazing attitude. I learned from him that everyday we have the choice to live fully.

There are as many different stories about life situations as there are people. Some situations seem much worse than others and some situations seem trivial. The different situations that we all deal with on a daily basis are called life!

What we know today is that each of us have much more influence on life and what happens in our world than we ever thought possible. It's the old cause and effect thing and it all comes down to the choices we make. You can choose to think positive, happy thoughts, or you can choose to wallow in self pity as a victim of outside influences that you have nothing to do with.

The Self Esteem Issue

I have included a little section on self esteem because it is one of the single most powerful influences in a person's life. Self esteem is what you think about yourself. What value do you put on yourself? How do you rate yourself? It's not about what others think of you, it is about what you think of yourself!

Often times, people are brought down by those around them. In many cases, it is family member, a significant other or even a close friend that will influence and affect someone else's self esteem in a negative way. Why someone would want to do that to another person is beyond me. Perhaps this approach merely covers their own insecurities. Some derive self importance and power from the feeling that they control another person.

More times than not the root of a poor self esteem can be traced directly back to how we were raised as young children. However, we can't afford to cling to the belief/fact that we had a bad upbringing to account for all our thoughts and esteem issues as adults. Part of being an adult is the ability to review our life as children and determine if there were adverse conditions that might have affected our self esteem or any other vital motivations. If there are we must deal with these issues in a way that we are no longer held hostage by a childhood we cannot change. It is our choice to deal with the past and begin to build a new future to become the person we want to be.

Often, it is those with a low self-esteem that easily fall into the "victim trip" syndrome. It is not uncommon to find that women in abusive relationships fall into this category. It may not appear to the person themselves or to the world at large that a particular person might have a low self esteem as some are able to mask it well to both themselves and the outside world.

Abuse—Choice—Self Esteem

Think about this for just a minute. In America, a woman is battered every 15 seconds and two to four million are abused each year, yet most of these woman don't report it and they stay in the relationship. By the way, it's their choice to stay in the relationship!

More times than not, they will rationalize their decision for one reason or another. Perhaps they believe it was their fault that they were beaten or perhaps they are willing to tolerate it for the sake of the children. Any reason is WRONG, WRONG, WRONG! There is NO valid reason to tolerate abuse especially when it escalates to the level of physical violence.

For those that choose to stay and tolerate physical abuse for any reason here's a scary fact from the American Psychological Association. Forty to sixty percent of men that abuse woman also abuse children. So, if someone you know is hiding behind the "it's for the sake of the children" excuse, it's time to face the real truth. To stay in an abusive relationship for the children's sake is emotionally and mentally traumatic and may ultimately harm the very children they are trying to protect.

It is often times a low self esteem that allows a woman to stay in an abusive relationship. In this country, just over three women per day are being murdered by their partners. This year in America, approximately 4,000 women will die as a result of domestic violence. In 2001, approximately 588,490 women and 82,400 men were the subject of reported non-fatal domestic violence.

The time to do something about domestic violence is right now. **It's a choice!** There is lots of help available and it's a matter of mental, physical emotional and spiritual health. In many cases, it may be a matter of life and death.

There are many places to turn for help. One can usually start with their own church or religion. Some large employers offer confidential, in-house, counseling, and of course there is the internet. I would suggest a site, www.FaithTrustInstitute.org for additional information, articles, and where to go for help. In any event, this is serious stuff and the outcome is solely based on the choice that you make. If you know someone in an abusive relationship you can't decide for them, but you can let them know there is help out there and that you are there for them.

If someone you know doesn't believe that they have the personal power to make whatever choices about life that they want, they may have low self-esteem. Here's that old cliché again: "This is the first day of the rest of your life." It's true. We all have fresh and new choices to make each and every day.

It's the choices that we make each day that define who we are. It's these choices that express our character to the world; it's these choices that provide for the passion in our life.

Now that we know we control all our daily choices, we have to look at our mission, plan and overall goal. These directives should influence and provide automatic input into the choices we make. If we are making choices without knowing what the real personal mission, plan or goal is, we are assured of not reaching any of them and probably never really being happy in life.

As funny as it may sound, many of us travel through life without clear direction. Oh, in the back of our minds, we have an idea what or where we'd like to be in some certain amount of time, we just don't have a real clear vision of how it will unfold. Most of us don't have any sort of written plan or even a personal mission statement about ourselves.

As a part of this chapter, it is a must to spend some time on what choices we have personally made and what ones we are making every day about our lives.

In one of the programs I conduct, "It's My Life, Who's in Charge," I recommend that the participants set aside the better part of a week to give thought to what is really important in their lives (an hour or two per day). This would include both personal and business issues. On the personal side, my belief is that an individual must give time and energy to this by themselves first prior to sharing it with their spouse.

Although a personal mission may well include a spouse, significant other, children, or other family members or even a very close friend, a personal mission and personal identity are really a very, very personal choice. It is the essence of who you are and what you reflect to yourself and the universe.

The beautiful thing about having free will and having choices in life is that nobody can tell us who we are, it's our choice. Sometimes we may be pressured by our family or friends to act in certain ways. The real questions are: Who am I? What do I want in life? What will I contribute in life? Once some consideration and clarity have been given to a personal mission, it's wonderful to share them with a person that you love and admire.

In respect to a business plan or career moves, it's a must to get buy-in from your significant other as it can be extremely difficult to succeed without the support of your own household.

The line between personal and business is now blurred more than ever before as technology and the information era make no distinction as to where or when the time clock is punched, if it's punched at all. More and more people have or are in the process of dismissing the notion altogether that there is any line between personal and business. As more and more people operate "home based businesses", or have moved into a service or information based career and away from punching the clock the less the separation line is evident.

In most cases, the personal mission statement is more likely the "who" we are that defines our character whereas the business mission will probably reflect the "what we do" for a living. It's a wonderful bonus when the lines blur because we are doing for a living exactly what we want to do!

Choice is Exciting!

Regardless where we've been both physically and mentally in our past, the choices that we have the opportunity to make today and tomorrow is what makes life interesting and exciting.

Many of us have referred to an individual in conversation by saying, "Boy, does she have potential" or we might be discussing the attributes of our own children with pride and an indication of what they will be doing with their lives, again this is based on potential. Potential is a wonderful thing as we all have it. Whether we reach our full potential is clearly defined by the choices we make on a daily basis.

It's clear that the key word in self-esteem is "self." In short, we have the choice concerning how we feel about ourself, we have the personal power to alter our "self" and we do that by the choices we make.

As you flow through this guide-book, a formula to move from one level to another should be clearly unfolding. The motivational checklist in the previous chapter when completed clarifies the real and sincere desire that will drive the choices you make.

Some people have never seen themselves in a leadership role in their life, or as the person responsible for making major life choices. The next chapter is about the leadership role that each of us plays in our life. It is a chapter about empowerment. It's the final step in making change!

Notes/Ideas

Chapter 5

Leadership Role

Are you a leader or a follower? The truth is you are both. It's worthwhile to take a close look at leadership qualities and to determine how and where you fit into the leadership role.

The philosophical concept about life that comes with the leadership role is: **It's our life therefore we are in charge!**

In this guide, we are talking about life and some commonsense strategies that clarify and simplify the decision making process while at the same time increasing and improving the essence of life itself.

So, here is the truth: **It's our life therefore we are in charge!**

We are the decision makers about what's going to happen.

We are the responsible party for our own actions.

We decide whether to have a fulfilling life or a wasted one.

We decide whether to spend our emotional dollars on love or on hate. We decide whether we will be happy or sad.

We decide how we will react to what life throws our way.

We select the direction we will follow in life.

We select the people we choose to call friends.

We select our own significant other.

We determine when we have made a mistake.

We are responsible for changing our direction when we want change.

We are the sole person responsible for this very important life!

We are the leader!

Since it is our life and there is no realistic or practical way out of the ultimate responsibility for it, it's probably a good time to talk about the leadership role that has been thrust upon us.

While it would be prudent and reasonable to take charge of this responsibility, we have all seen people that have not taken a leadership role in their own lives. There are certainly many people that don't take responsibility for their own lives. Often times we refer to them as those that are on a "victim trip." It's interesting that a person can convince themselves that they are not responsible for the position they find themselves in, in life. In fact, many times I find it quite entertaining to actually listen to this type of "victim" although I usually can't take them for long.

Let's clarify the traits we are referring to in the victim. It is the way that they react to the situation they find themselves that causes us to classify them, not necessarily the situation they are in. We can all find ourselves in awkward or bad situations that we had little control over such as going to war or being blind-sided by a drunk driver. The point is how we deal with the adversity, do we take on the poor me I'm a victim role, or do we act with character and fight with courage.

How we react to adversity in our lives is a statement about us not the adversity. We've seen leaders over the centuries react to adversity in different ways at different times; however, the single common element that they all displayed was the taking of the responsibility for their actions. That's one of the things that leaders do!

Those on a victim trip tend to not be responsible for their own situations. They typically don't acknowledge that they have the power to pick and choose their own reality. We have all felt sorry for ourselves on occasion and we have all found ourselves in a "rut" from time to time. It isn't helpful to beat ourselves up over it, but rather...get over it!

Included below is an article which was written for a January issue of *Success Magazine*, a magazine for sales professionals. It may shed some thoughts about getting out of a rut.

Am I in a Rut?

It's time to dig out.

It's at this time of year all across the northeast and mid-west part of the country that people are digging out of the snow on a daily basis.

They don't like it although they do it, daily if necessary, because it is simply part of the norm in their routines.

We often times slip into ruts in our sales business and our personal lives. In most cases, we're not aware that we are gradually slipping into a rut of sorts until we are well into the rut and much unproductive and unsatisfying time is being invested, on a daily basis, into a routine that yields little return.

It has been said many times that the definition of insanity is: Doing the same thing that you have always done and expecting a different outcome! Well for the most part, that is insanity and yet we all fall into this rut from time to time.

Automobiles typically want their oil changed every 3,000 to 5,000 miles along with a major tune-up around once a year. We require some simple maintenance as well to operate at or near peak levels. One of the check-ups that we should perform on a quarterly basis is the "Rut-Check." (I refer to it as the "Gut-Check")

It's a simple check-up which only requires a pencil, a small, inexpensive notebook or a piece of paper and about an hour of quiet and private time once a quarter. This time should be scheduled when one is alert, alone and will not be interrupted.

During this quiet time, there are three areas and/or questions that must be honestly addressed.

This "Rut-Check" consists of questions relating to Attitude, Motivation and Choices. It's best if a person can almost get outside of themselves, so to speak, to conduct this evaluation. Nobody knows you better than you, thus, if you can be totally honest with yourself, you can usually get a pretty good analysis as a result of this exercise.

Assume for the hour that you are stepping outside of yourself and that you have been hired as a consultant to look back at yourself and put on paper the answers to the following questions. Be honest!

1. Attitude:

How is my attitude right now?
Am I happy about what I'm doing?
Is my attitude good in my personal life?
Is it good in my business life?
Am I more positive about things or negative?
Why am I negative?
What could I do about it?

2. Motivation:

Am I motivated to excel?
Am I excited to get up each morning?
Am I motivated regarding my significant other?
Am I reading books daily?
Do I have written goals?
Am I excited about being alive?

3. Choices:

Have I been making good choices recently?
Am I aware that I have choices which can change my life daily?
Do I have the choice to do and be whatever I wish?
Am I carrying some emotional baggage that I won't let go of?
Am I choosing to put obstacles in my own way?

One should be able to answer these questions with some notes in about 30 to 40 minutes.

The balance of the hour, 20 to 30 minutes, is to get ourselves back on track. Perhaps with some written notes as to where we are going and how that relates to our over-all plan.

The bigger question comes up when we do this exercise and realize that we don't have an over-all plan. If we don't have an over-all plan or at least a personal mission statement to guide us in our direction, we will most certainly feel lost much of the time simply because we don't know where we are going!

Putting the plan together starts with knowing one's personal goals and reducing such things to writing. This article was designed to help you do a "Rut-Check".

If you have invested in a small notebook ($2.00), date and keep this analysis in the book and pull it out quarterly each time you complete your "Rut-Check". The ability to reflect back on previous quarters helps you analyze whether you are falling into the same rut over and over. This is also a great book to keep or jot down your new ideas. Until next month, dig out of the snow and dig out of the rut. Happy New Year!

(Reprinted with permission of Success Magazine, written by: J.C. Melvin)

Generally, people that get into ruts and stay there are not leaders. One of the qualities that leaders have is vision. In order for us to have vision, we must constantly refresh our point of view.

What Leadership is Not!

1. Leadership is NOT being the boss.
2. Management is not leadership.
3. Authority
4. Parenting
5. Having Power

Leadership is not necessarily being the boss, or the manager, or the one with authority or power to make changes. Parents are not always leaders. Leaders think of the greater good and act accordingly whether it means taking a risk or not.

We all have the inherent responsibility to manage ourselves. The ability to manage is an honorable thing and management of teams, people, systems and/or processes is a necessary thing. Here we will take a brief look at the basic differences between management and leadership.

■ Leaders think longer term

The leader's long term thinking means they tend to work well beyond the "daily crisis" mode. They are always focused beyond the immediate issue or crisis by looking longer term.

They see beyond their own unit

Their ability to see and influence beyond their own unit is a unique quality for the leader. They are able to see their part and relationship in the big picture of the larger realities.

They influence beyond their own unit

The leader's heavy influence on vision and values and other intangibles is what helps him or her effectively interact and communicate with others including any followers. Because leaders are focused on the greater good, the results of their units work impacts others in the workplace or community well outside of their unit.

Leaders place a heavy emphasis on vision

Vision, values and intangibles are very crisp and clear from the leader's point of view while others may not see things with such clarity and may only see "gray".

When I use the term "gray," I am referring to that abstract area of thought and creativity that is generally disregarded by pessimists, analytical thinkers, and scientists as unfounded theory and meaningless gibberish. The analytical likes things to be black or white, right or wrong, up or down. The truth is, so do most of us; however, life and leadership is not that simple much of the time.

To be fair to the analytical types, not all vision and values are gray as many visions and many values can be clearly defined and reduced to writing. It's when we focus on the "intangibles" and we begin to dissect emotional reasoning and emotional based vision and value that we enter into the "gray area".

Whether leaders are hard core analytical types or not, quality leaders clearly understand that there is a gray area in life and in the understanding of life. Quality leaders are able to look at the same situation from different points of view!

■ They have political skills

Most leaders possess good to great communication skills. In some cases, it may have come to them more naturally than in other cases. They tend to make us feel comfortable when they communicate with us.

■ **Leaders think change**

Leaders would typically be considered open-minded. They are open to change and new concepts. They grasp the concept of, "if you are not growing, you are dying."

Back to the Leadership Role!

So, as we look at various aspects of the "leadership role" and how we each have a part in the leadership role of our own lives, we're forced to draw several conclusions.

1. We are the leader in charge
2. If we're not leading, nobody's leading
3. If we don't pay attention, nobody will
4. If we're not motivated, it's our responsibility

And last but certainly not least, if we need to have a serious conversation with someone about taking charge, we'd be best served by pulling up a chair in front of a mirror and dealing with the person who keeps staring back at us!

One of the little known qualities of a leader is the ability to manage the meaning of change. I've left this for last because I feel it is one of the single most important qualities of a leader and yet is the quality most commonly skipped, or overlooked completely.

Whether it was 1963 with the assassination, in Dallas, of John F. Kennedy, the President of the United States or the terrorist attacks on New York City and Washington, DC on September 11th, 2001, we're all a part of an ever-changing world. Now-a-days it seems difficult to understand why certain things happen let alone comprehend the effect they will have on our lives.

Managing the meaning of change means that we are able to look at things that are happening every day and with an open mind see the subtle changes taking place. We are able to, with a fair degree of reasonableness, understand what the changes mean and what impact they have on our family and society. More than this, managing the meaning of change, means dealing with major tragedy and major events without losing control. Leaders have the ability to diagnose what it means, understand its effect on society (both short term and long term) and have the ability to relay in a down to earth way the change and effect to others.

As you might imagine, in order to be effective at managing the meaning of change, one must have the ability to set aside or at least take control of the emotionalism that clouds reasonable thinking. There is nothing wrong with being emotional except that it sometimes gets in the way of simple logical thinking.

Very emotional people can be and are great leaders all over the globe. Most have, through a growing up process, learned that when the time comes, they must set aside any uncontrolled emotion to draw valid meaning from change. Once the logical thinking process has been completed and diagnosed, it can then be relayed to our children, family and co-workers.

Whatever the situation, tragedy or other major event, most people are looking for a leader to tell them that everything is going to be alright. It's the same thing that parents do with their young children when they fall down. They tell them that everything will be O.K. They clean them up and instill them with confidence again. That's what parents do and that's what leaders do!

Whatever your background, career, or current status is in life, you have the opportunity to take on the leadership role with respect to your life and future. We are all leaders in life, and we have an effect on all those who come into our lives.

Embracing the concept of managing the meaning of change is key to keeping yourself (as the leader) open minded about what happens in the world. Understanding this responsibility to yourself and those around you stops you from reacting in a childlike way to new and different situations.

What's Next?

Through this guide you have completed a self evaluation, done an attitude check and now understand that we are all motivated. You know how to move motivation in a more positive direction should you have the sincere desire to do so. You are clear that what happens today and every day is the result of the choices you make. You have learned to let go of baggage that is not benefiting you and find the positive in past experiences you cannot change. You are clear that you are a leader and the one in charge.

In the final chapter, it's time to make it all come together!

Notes/Ideas

Chapter 6

Putting It All Together!

Although putting it all together is the closing chapter of this guide-book, I sincerely hope it will be the beginning of magnificent change!

It is my hope that you found these pages helpful whether you are one of the fortunate that is currently in MPES balance and on track, looking to tweak a few things or you are in search of major change. In any event, use the formula as a catalyst to stimulate change and growth in every thing you do.

Remember, the secret ingredient, if there is one in this recipe, is ACTION! Based on the chapters and the formula for creating change, the list below is the logical order and process to occasionally review and maintain the forward movement of action. It is a formula to both accomplish goals and live the dream. We have got to keep in mind that life is not a destination...it is a journey to be enjoyed!

Addressing the Why and the What!

1. Is there a want for change in your life?

    a. It could be massive change or simply growth.

    b. What is the desire?

2. Where are you now and what's the starting point?

    a. This requires a written self assessment; you can't go anywhere meaningful without knowing where you are today!

    b. See chapter one, self awareness, for the questions to answer.

3. How is your attitude?

    a. You must do an honest evaluation of it and take action, if necessary.

    b. Chapter two is about understanding why our attitudes are the way they are and taking action to change them if desired.

    c. Do you need to deal with any emotional baggage from your past? If so, now is the time.

4. You must evaluate and identify your motivation level.

    a. We are all motivated; the charge is to be sure we are motivated in a positive direction.

    b. Chapter three deals with unlocking the motivation within and moving it in a more positive direction.

    c. One must be clear on their sincere desires in life to accomplish this part of the task. This is the "dare to dream" part of the formula!

5. Each of us must take charge of ourselves and make choices which reflect our character.

a. If necessary, we must re-define our character and grow our level of self esteem.

b. We must be clear on who we are!

6. Having used the straight forward approach to resolve past baggage and identify not only where we are but who we are, it's time to take the ultimate leadership role in life, responsibility of self.

Is it Really that Simple?

I suppose we can use our superior intelligence to complicate any issue in life. Part of the entire living experience is the constant asking of questions. The most common question is why? We can ask the "why" question in every conceivable way and then wait for some one or some being to answer the question and/or justify the reason why!

Life is simple

Providing we are honest with ourselves, the only why that we can really ever answer with certainty is the why we did something, or the why we feel a certain way, or think a certain way. We have control and responsibility for ourselves. Our thoughts and actions have an effect on our family members and all those we come in contact with throughout our lives. No man or woman is an island and each of us brings to the table of life a complete buffet of thoughts, love, emotion, ideas and character!

When the meal of life is over and the spirits talk, laugh and discuss the different parts of the buffet, what will they say about the items that you personally contributed to the buffet of life?

More important than that, how will you personally evaluate your contribution to the planet and universe?

The frog in the pot of hot water did not realize that a threat existed and his instinct was not enough to tell him to jump out until it was too late.

We are a different creature and we always have a choice. We have the choice to create and live any dream we can imagine.

Create your dream...and start living it today!

Notes/Ideas

Acknowledgments

A special thanks to my wife, Minnie, for her encouragement, ideas and what seemed to me to be pleasant nagging throughout the writing of this book. It is with her support of me and her belief in me that this book truly comes together.

I would be remiss if I did not give a special thanks to my editor, Annie Johnston, who tolerated me and taught me throughout the writing and production of this book.

Thanks Minnie and thanks Annie, I love you both.

I would also like to acknowledge the hundreds of thousands of independent sales people that work every day to provide for themselves and their families. Most of these men and women are paid by commission only based on the sales they make. It is truly these folks that work in the trenches of life which plays mind games with your attitude and motivation.

I'd like to acknowledge all those that strive to better themselves on a daily basis. The world is abundant with greatness.

It is however, those believers that take action in their truth and dreams that bring that greatness to life. Thank you for believing in yourself, you're awesome.

Lastly, thank you Sally for always being there, you are the definition of friendship..

J. C.'s Recommended Reading

Below are several books that I have found to be well written and inspirational. Each may stimulate change in a person's point of view, life or career by reading them.

The Traveler's Gift, Seven Decisions That Determine Personal Success by Andy Andrews. Easy read, insightful, inspiring and focused on a positive attitude. **A MUST READ!**

The Lost Choice, A Legend of Personal Discovery by Andy Andrews. This Parable is about the hidden potential of the human heart. Very inspiring!

If "I Think I Smell Garlic" was able to help you in the direction you want to go and you are looking for a more detailed formula, then I'd suggest: *The Motivated MIND, A Complete Guide to Personal Change* by J. M. Gracia.

Because I speak to so many real estate sales people, this recommendation is directed to them. The book and system have nothing to do with any particular real estate company. It was written by three men of knowledge and experience. I feel fortunate to know two of the writers personally and recommend: *The Millionaire Real Estate Agent* by Gary Keller with Dave Jenks and Jay Papasan.

Lastly, I would recommend a small and easy to read book about being different, *Purple Cow*. Whether you have interest in marketing, business or just life and getting outside the box the author, Seth Godin, opens the door of creativity for any to walk through.

The "Garlic Press" Newsletter

Don't forget to sign up for J.C.'s motivational Newsletter at
JCMelvin.com

" I Think I Smell Garlic" Recipe

Just in case anyone might still be thinking this is a cookbook, I thought I'd include one of my favorite recipes:

Linguini with White Clam Sauce! *(for two)*

Ingredients

13 oz. of chopped clams
  (two 6 ½ cans of snows)
  with clam juice
Fresh parsley
Fresh or dried basil &
  crushed red pepper
Fresh garlic or bottled diced
  or crushed garlic

Chicken broth
White wine (any kind)
¼ lb unsalted butter cube
Olive oil
½ fresh lemon
½ pound linguini
Parmesan Cheese

First cook ½ lb. linguini to desired texture and set aside in strainer at sink.

With a 10- to 16-inch sauce pan put two tablespoons of olive oil and turn to medium heat. While heating, open the cans of clams with clam juice. When skillet is warmed, add ½ to 1 teaspoon of chopped garlic. Garlic should simmer slowly, not to burn. As garlic just begins to brown at all, add ½ cup of white wine. Roll wine in pan to assist in evaporation and immediately add the clams with juice. Stir in and bring to a low simmer. Add one cup of chicken broth, two dashes of basil, one to three dashes of crushed red pepper, and squeeze in juice of ½ lemon. Allow to reduce by 20 to 30 percent in volume. Lastly cut the ¼ lb. butter cube into 4 pieces and place all pieces into simmering recipe, turn up heat slightly to cause a low boiling effect while stirring in the butter as you go. This will cause sauce to thicken.

Place cooked linguini in strainer under running hot water to reheat pasta. Place pasta in bowls or on plates. As sauce thickens add diced fresh parsley to sauce, stir in...pour sauce and clams over pasta and finish with a bit more fresh parsley over top of pasta...Sprinkle with Parmesan or make available tableside. Enjoy!